NEXT
GENERATION
REAL ESTATE

J. LENNOX SCOTT

SHELLEY ROSSI

ISBN 1-886225-82-6
Cover design by Angie Johnson

Library of Congress Control Number: 2002100955

Dageforde Publishing, Inc.
128 East 13th Street
Crete, Nebraska 68333
www.dageforde.com

Printed in the United States of America
10 9 8 7 6 5 4 3 2 1

Contents

PREFACE

Real estate is facilitated *by* people on *behalf* of people. It is a relationship centric business model that has stood the test of time because of the intrinsic value that we as real estate professionals bring to the transaction. With that being said, it is imperative for us to always move forward by keeping abreast of our customer's needs and the changes taking place in the world around us. *Next Generation Real Estate* does just that.

There's never been a more exciting time to be in real estate, and thanks to the Internet, the next generation of real estate is filled with infinite possibilities for brokers, agents and clients alike. To be successful in *next generation real estate,* it's important to be aware of the changes that are taking place in the real estate profession and to act accordingly. Now, more than ever, real estate is about much more than helping people buy and sell homes; it's about the important relationship that exists between agents and their clients. There are endless opportunities to enhance this relationship by using *customer relationship management* and *real time real estate.*

Real time real estate is based upon the idea that everything in real estate is instant—instant communication, instant marketing, and instant information. Success in next generation real estate relies on this concept of *real time* everything—using tools, such as the Internet. The process isn't simple, nor is it inexpensive, but the concepts discussed in *Next Generation Real Estate* will help empower real estate professionals to accomplish more for themselves and their clients than was ever imaginable before.

Next Generation Real Estate also discusses techniques to help agents improve the quality of their lives. It's all too common in this industry for real estate agents to burn out. It shouldn't be about success at any price, but rather about success within a balanced life. Brokers must partner with their agents to attain a healthy balance and be successful. *Next Generation Real Estate* discusses ways to enable agents to double their productivity while maintaining healthy balanced lives.

Ultimately, my approach is from that of the independent real estate broker, but the philosophies discussed in *Next Generation Real Estate* can apply to all real estate professionals regardless of the size or ownership of the company you work for. My priority is to develop a business model that focuses on two practices: enhancing the home ownership experience and enhancing the agent experience. And technology plays an integral role in both. In many ways the two are actually one and the same because many of the tools and practices that improve the homebuyer/seller's experience improve the agent's experience too, and visa versa. It is these systems and this approach to real estate that define *Next Generation Real Estate*.

ACKNOWLEDGMENTS

There are a number of people whom I would like to thank for their support and contributions to *Next Generation Real Estate*. First and foremost to be acknowledged are my grandfather, John L. Scott, and my father, W. Lennox Scott, who is truly my hero. As leaders, both men were very dedicated to this business and they are responsible for laying the foundation for the philosophies and culture at John L. Scott Real Estate.

Thanks also go to the John L. Scott team, both past and present, for carrying the torch for John L. Scott. I simply see myself as the team's spokesperson—the team members are the ones who make this company successful and who make it possible to continually implement next generation real estate.

I would also like to recognize several people who have contributed to this book in many ways: First is real estate extraordinaire, Terri Murphy. Terri has been extremely helpful and supportive in my efforts to complete *Next Generation Real Estate*. Her insight and direction were invaluable and extremely appreciated.

I'd like to thank Steve Murray, president of Murray Consulting and co-editor of *REAL Trends*, for his friendship and support over the years and for his contribution to *Next Generation Real Estate.*

I would like to acknowledge my friend, Roald Marth, CEO of WhereToLive.com. Roald helped develop the concepts for real time real estate, which contributed greatly to the development of *Next Generation Real Estate.*

Thank you to Jerry Moon, executive vice president of John L. Scott Real Estate. Jerry has been instrumental in the growth and success of John L. Scott over the last twelve years. Among other things, Jerry is responsible for the development of our transaction service center, one of the fundamentals for success in next generation real estate.

Finally, a big thanks to John L. Scott Real Estate public relations director, Shelley Rossi. Shelley was the writer for *Next Generation Real Estate.* Her enthusiasm is contagious, and her understanding and interpretation of the concepts in *Next Generation Real Estate* were invaluable. It was a joy to work with Shelley and to make a difference in the real estate industry with her.

In closing, I would like to express my love for my children, DJ, Stephanie and Savannah, who are truly the joys of my life. And to my Mom for her love and support throughout my life.

1

REAL TIME REAL ESTATE

The real estate industry continues to evolve in new exciting directions, largely due to the role the Internet has played in the business. This is the most exciting time in the history of real estate because everything is changing as it remains the same. What's changing is the process; what remains the same is the trusted relationship that exists between the agent and client.

There are endless opportunities to enhance this very important relationship by using what is called *real time real estate*.

Real time is the only time. It's now, it's instant, and it's all about offering the ultimate level of customer service. In real time, what formerly took three or four days now takes only seconds, thanks to the Internet. The Internet is the greatest communication, information, productivity—and now—relationship tool in the history of real estate. The Internet has empowered real estate companies to provide instant marketing and communication, significantly enhancing customer service, the transaction processes and productivity.

Success in next generation real estate relies on the concept of *real time everything*. Agents are competing more than ever for clients, forcing them to demonstrate the value that sets them apart from the rest. The Internet gives them the ability to do this.

Real time real estate requires continual investment and reinvestment to be successful. The process isn't simple, nor is it inexpensive, but ultimately, real estate agents are empowered to accomplish more for themselves and their clients than was ever imaginable before.

Real time real estate can be applied to every aspect of the business, from buying and selling to living in the home. It impacts the entire real estate transaction process and all who are involved. The methods involved in real time real estate empower agent/client relationships, resulting in highly satisfied clients as well as repeat and referral business.

Real Time Marketing

It's commonly known that the first two weeks that a home is on the market are the most important. This is because there is always a backlog of potential buyers, currently working with agents, who are eager to view new properties the instant they come onto the market. Once two weeks have passed and the backlog of buyers has seen the home, traffic reduces significantly. From this point on, the home is typically shown to one buyer at a time as they enter the market place, greatly decreasing the potential for a sale. In fact, once the first two weeks have passed, the chances for a sale are reduced by one-half for every month the home is on the market. Furthermore, if a home does not sell within the first two weeks, the market has spoken which usually means that the seller will need to make some adjustments in home condition or price to secure a sale. That is why real time real estate is vital—it gives agents access to systems that enable them to market their listings *day one.*

Day One Marketing

Real time marketing requires agents to use tools such as the Internet to sell homes more quickly. Agents have one shot at real time marketing, and that's why it's so important for an agent to start marketing day one on the company web site. Many Multiple Listing Services are now web based, enabling agents to upload multiple photos of the home as they input their listing information. This process is even more critical in those areas that practice *Broker Reciprocity* (also referred to as IDX as discussed in chapter 3). The value of posting photos of listings on the Internet cannot be stressed enough. Without a photo, the online listing is extremely ineffective. When customers go online to search for homes, they want to see photos. It has been proven time and time again that potential buyers will pass right by a listing without photos.

Furthermore, agents who are not utilizing the power of photos are not doing an effective job for their sellers. Photos attract more agents and more buyers. Photos increase the chance of a sale, and ultimately, increase business and earnings for the real estate agent and the company. A full explanation of the systems necessary to successfully utilize the real time marketing process will be discussed in chapter 2.

Real Time Communications

Over the last several years, the real estate industry has been moving technologically toward real time through the use of fax machines, pagers, computers, cellular phones, voicemail, email, the Internet, and now wireless email and PDAs. Each of these items works independently and in tandem to enhance the communication process, allowing agents to practice real time real estate.

To maximize the potential of real time real estate, agents need faster Internet connections, such as DSL high-speed access, both at the office and at home. Agents also need tools, such as wireless email, wireless laptop computers and other forms of technology that adapt to their work environment. Real estate agents rarely sit behind a desk; they spend most of their time in the field, and they need technology that enables them to communicate effectively from the field. In other words, they need to be *Agent Now*.

Agent Now refers to the real estate industry's response to a customer's desire for instant communication. If it's not instant, it's not fast enough. Same day phone calls and emails are crucial to this business because customers don't want to wait for correspondence. They want Agent Now. And if they are forced to wait, chances are they will be lost as clients. Everyone knows the saying, "The early bird gets the worm." The saying holds true for real estate too. "The early agent gets the client." Customers have intent, so when they initiate contact, whether it's via telephone or email, agents must respond instantly— the quicker, the better. It's the client's expectation.

REAL TIME REAL ESTATE

The real estate industry is constantly criticized for not promptly returning voice or email messages, but the truth of the matter is that agents spend so much time in the field that the Agent Now concept has been very challenging for many of them. John L. Scott, the founder of John L. Scott Real Estate, believed that success in the real estate business relied on completing the circle of communication. He used to say that you should return every phone call immediately, even if you don't have an answer, because it provides that customer with a level of satisfaction and it completes the initial circle of communication. Immediate response appeases the client while giving the agent additional time to obtain requested information. The same approach can be used with email.

Responding to phone calls throughout the workday is a good way to avoid a backlog of messages at the day's end. Cellular phones have been of great assistance in this area because they have enabled agents to respond quickly to client calls. However, it's important to remember that the cellular phone has a power button, and it should be used during personal time. It's a good idea to batch phone calls and email messages to make the most efficient use of time.

The Internet has created an environment in which people want and expect the fastest response possible. This reinforces the importance of implementing communication solutions for agents. In order to meet the client's expectations, next generation real estate agents need to communicate using tools, such as wireless email, through advanced systems that allow them to create a virtual office while they're out in the field. By practicing real time real estate, agents are able to use their time more efficiently, be more productive, and more effectively complete the circle of communication with their clients.

Internet Home Buyers

Buyers who use the Internet to assist them during a home search are referred to as Internet buyers. And research shows that a real estate agent spends half as much time during a sale with Internet buyers as with non-Internet buyers. Internet buyers help make the real estate process more efficient. They use the Internet to educate themselves in the fine points of the home buying process, and they're entirely open to using email and other online advancements. By the time Internet buyers connect with a real estate agent, they are highly motivated, well informed, and ready to move through the home buying process. Furthermore, buyers who use the Internet have a better idea of what they want. They typically know the style of home, the price range, the neighborhood(s), mortgage payments, and— chances are—they probably already know of several homes that fit within their search parameters.

Home buyers have a high level of energy when they're searching for a home. The Internet provides a place for home owners to channel this energy and enhances their home buying experience. Real estate is buyer activated approximately 85 percent of the time. With this in mind, the goal should be to adapt technology to home buyer behavioral patterns. For example, one thing that can always be counted on with home buyers is the *drive by*. Buyers will always drive around neighborhoods looking for homes that meet their personal parameters, a behavior that hasn't changed over the years and probably never will. In fact, statistics show that about 25 percent of home buyers find the home they end up buying by driving around (Hebert Research, 2000). In order to adapt technology to this behavior, all real estate companies should advertise their web address on their sale signage. Then, as buyers drive by a home in which they are interested, they see the web address and are drawn to the Internet for more information. The result is a potential visitor to that company's web site, as well as a potential client and sale.

Research shows that 11 percent of buyers first see the home they end up buying on the Internet (Hebert Research, 2000). Research has also shown that 96.6 percent of homebuyers, including those who did not use the Internet previously, say they will use the Internet during their next home purchase. It is also worth noting that 90 percent of John L. Scott Real Estate homebuyers are already using the Internet during their home searches, which clearly demonstrates the enormous potential the web can have for all real estate companies. With further expansion of the Internet, faster computer processors and improved, high-speed connections, current numbers will continue to rise substantially. In fact, it's predicted that by 2006, 41 percent of households will have advanced high speed Internet access, making the Internet even more of an integral part of every buyer's home search.

Real Estate Is Buyer Activated

But what about the majority of home buyers—the other 89 percent that doesn't find the home they end up buying on the Internet? The goal is not necessarily to have every single buyer finding that dream home online. The point is to understand that the real estate market is buyer activated. And communities are in perpetual motion because of the movement of buyers. This concept can be visualized by imagining the scenario captured by a time lapse camera from five miles above the ground. There would be a continuous movement through the community of first-time buyers, moving from apartments into homes; people selling their homes to move into other homes; people relocating into and out of various communities.

It is important to understand that communities, and therefore the real estate market, are in perpetual motion, driven by home buyers. It's a continuous cycle that takes place every minute of every day.

Real estate clients are migrating to the Internet to seek home buying information at a very rapid pace. It's vitally important that real estate companies stay one step ahead by implementing real time real estate—or risk the chance of losing those clients to the companies that are already doing so.

2

PERSONALIZED SERVICE ENHANCED WITH TECHNOLOGY

Information Source Marketing

Next generation real estate strengthens business by creating and using the ultimate web site, complete with unique web addresses for every listing, Internet listing demonstrations, virtual tours, and audio descriptions—all of which are elements of information source marketing. Agents win listings, meet buyers, earn referrals, and enhance their client's experience by becoming relationship focused and technologically empowered through the use of information source marketing. It's no longer an option, but rather a necessity for real estate companies to provide the latest online advances. They eventually will not be able to compete for agents or for clients without them. It is through these online advances that companies are able to effectively practice information source marketing, which is a very important aspect of next generation real estate.

It is extremely worthwhile to invest in information source marketing because it enables companies to establish themselves—and their agents—as the first point of relationship. If successful, information source marketing is an extremely effective way to attract and secure customers. One of the best ways to facilitate information source marketing is through technology. When people start looking for a home, they enter the investigation stage full of intent. This intent is like an open invitation to real estate companies and agents to supply them with information. Real estate companies need to tap into that intent in order to attract those buyers to their agents and their business. The many effective ways of doing this will be discussed in detail in this chapter, but the ultimate message is that next generation real estate companies must use technology to capture a buyer's intent in order to secure them as a customer.

Interactive Voice Response

In 1990 one of the first examples of using technology to attract homebuyers during the investigation stage was developed. It was called Interactive Voice Response (IVR). At this same time, John L. Scott Real Estate developed its own IVR system called ScottLine®. ScottLine® is an interactive voice response system that allows customers to access information on specific homes in which they are interested by simply calling a toll-free telephone number and entering the property's individual five digit code. Every listing is assigned its own code which is clearly displayed on company signage and in newspaper advertising.

ScottLine® was very advanced for its time when it was introduced, causing some agents to be resistant to its function. The concern was that potential clients would no longer need to contact real estate agents when they wanted to access information about a home. These agents felt that their value was in the information they could provide buyers. However, the opposite was actually true. With ScottLine®, potential buyers were more qualified, better informed, and further along in the buying process by the time they contacted the agent.

IVR gave companies the opportunity to position themselves as the first point of relationship, acting as the *information source* for all buyers, including those who potentially would have chosen a different real estate company. In essence, companies using an IVR system went from being withholders of information to *information sources* for buyers, and this proved to be a very successful shift.

History of the Internet in Real Estate

Technology has changed drastically over the last several years, but customer behavioral patterns have essentially remained the same. People who are looking for a home have intent, and they want to seek out information on their own before they initiate contact with a real estate professional. In fact, most buyers go through the investigation stage before securing an agent, which for some may take only a few weeks while others might take several months. Buying a home is a very personal experience, and buyers typically initiate their own search process, illustrating that the entire real estate process is buyer activated.

During the investigation stage, buyers experience what can be called *euphoria weekend,* a process that involves driving around neighborhoods collecting information and researching the market. These buyers might also refer to the newspaper or real estate magazines for additional information. It has been proven time and again that buyers want the satisfaction of seeing potential homes and neighborhoods in person. This behavioral pattern is commonly known to real estate companies, but until recently, except for the use of flyer boxes, companies have not been marketing seriously to the buyer in the investigation stage. IVR was one of the first technological systems to operate as an information source for buyers in the investigation stage. But in 1993 that all changed thanks to the introduction of the Internet.

The Internet is truly the greatest marketing tool in the history of real estate. Beyond anything we could have ever imagined prior to 1993, the Internet has opened the window of opportunity in the areas of communication, service and information. The Internet allowed for the development and practice of real time real estate, and it is the underlying premise in everything involving next generation real estate.

By 1994, it was clear that the Internet was going to have enormous impact on the real estate industry. Because of this, a handful of companies including John L. Scott Real Estate wasted no time migrating their business online. By 1995 John L. Scott was the first company in the Pacific Northwest to post its entire listing inventory with photos on the Internet, allowing the company to market itself to buyers all around the world. During this same time, John L. Scott provided all its agents with high-speed Internet access in the offices, their own email addresses, and personal home pages. Knowing the agents needed a place to manage their home pages and online listings, John L. Scott created a company *intranet* site which included the resources that agents needed in order to be connected. Additionally, agents could connect to this integrated system from anywhere they had computer/Internet access, making it extremely convenient for them to input listings and photos in real time. As a result of these actions, John L. Scott was quickly becoming one of the first companies in real estate to market itself online—but that was not to last for long.

Flash forward seven years and now almost everyone and everything is online. The Internet acts as the centerpiece of everything that is done in real estate, enabling companies to provide information source marketing and to be the first point of relationship for prospective clients. The Internet has empowered agents to enhance the real estate customer's experience because they are now able to offer innovative online tools to help customers through the home buying and selling process.

Internet Property Link®

Buyers have clearly communicated to the real estate industry that when they have intent they want to see multiple photos and further information about properties they are potentially interested in buying. The Internet enables them to do so, twenty-four hours a day, seven days a week. Because of this, next generation real estate companies must implement programs that meet the needs of these buyers. Internet Property Link®, a program developed by John L. Scott Real Estate, does just this.

Internet Property Link® is an online program that assigns every John L. Scott listing a unique web address (i.e., www.johnlscott.com/12345). Customers simply key in the home's assigned web address and—voilà!—they go right to the listing. Here they have instant access to virtual tours, multiple photos, audio descriptions, open house information, mapping and much more. The agent's name and contact information are also listed as a reference for more information. Internet Property Link® goes far beyond interactive voice response, or any other marketing tool of its kind because it drives buyers to the Internet—specifically, *to John L. Scott's web site*. By this means, John L. Scott becomes the information source for those buyers and draws them into a relationship with the company and ultimately with a John L. Scott agent.

Newspaper Advertising and the Internet

The function that newspaper advertising plays in marketing a home has changed drastically since the introduction of the Internet. However, referring to the weekend real estate section of the newspaper continues to be an element of traditional buyer behavioral patterns. This is an important part of the process for many home buyers and has been throughout the history of real estate. Newspapers will continue to play a role in selling homes, but more as a function of driving buyers to the Internet. The truth is, newspapers simply cannot offer the same level of information or quality of visuals that the web can, and they can only show limited inventory. Furthermore, newspaper advertising is very costly and the return is not as great as that of the Internet. In many newspapers, the most read portion of the real estate section is "New on the Market" which lists properties that have recently been listed for sale. Keeping this in mind, companies should use this type of newspaper advertising in tandem with the Internet to target buyers.

There are those skeptics who suggest that the web will never replace newspaper advertising because of the number of people who still do not have Internet access. This statement might have some truth to it at the moment, but buyer demographics are quickly changing. Consider that 68 percent of homes with a household income of fifty thousand dollars a year have access to the Internet. In addition to this, 78 percent of homes that have a household income of seventy-five thousand dollars a year have access to the Internet, and the percentage only increases as household income increases.

Further statistical information that supports the importance of the Internet, states that 96.6 percent of recent home buyers surveyed in the Pacific Northwest said they plan to use the Internet during their next home purchase. It just goes to show that if a company invests in developing a functional web site with useful tools and information, the clients will come. For those clients who don't have Internet access or who aren't interested in using online tools, it's still important to offer traditional marketing programs. However, to be successful in next generation real estate, it's very important to understand that the Internet is where the future of the industry is headed—and where the customers are headed, too.

Email Notification of New Properties on the Market

Another innovative tool that came along because of the Internet is a program that allows real estate companies to notify buyers of new homes that come onto the market via email. This type of email program is becoming more commonplace as real estate companies recognize the valuable role it can play in providing information source marketing to customers on a continual basis.

At John L. Scott, the email notification program is called Home Delivery®. Home Delivery® is a personalized search tool that allows prospective buyers to enter their search parameters, including location, price range and other details. Then, as homes that meet their criteria come onto the market, the buyer is contacted by email. When buyers sign up for email notification programs they give companies permission to make contact with them about their real estate needs, on their terms. The customer reciprocates the contact when ready. Email notification programs add value to the agent's role because they enhance their clients' home search process. The program also greatly increases a company's pool of potential customers.

Online Open House Information

Another useful program that companies are beginning to offer on their web sites is online open house information. This feature enables agents to post open house information online so the public has access to area schedules at all times. Online open house information increases open house traffic, which ultimately provides further opportunities for agents to meet prospective clients.

As an example, at John L. Scott, a listing that has been identified as *open* by the agent, instantly appears in the "Open This Week" search area on the John L. Scott web site, making it extremely easy for visitors to locate open house information. Additionally, any listing that is "Open This Week" will be identified by a banner on that home's individual web page during the week leading up to the open house. Some companies also use email notification programs to provide home buyers with instant access to the most current open house information. This ultimately enhances the customer experience and adds value to the agents' service offerings because it simplifies the overall home search process.

Online Agent and Online Manager

Not only does Internet technology enhance the service agents are able to offer clients, it also establishes the agents and the companies they represent as technologically proficient. With the ever-increasing presence of the Internet, it's important to be able to market a business to the public as technologically advanced. Internet-empowered consumers want to know they are working with real estate professionals who have access to and who are proficient with the latest online innovations. Real estate companies are gradually catching onto this idea and are, therefore, developing ways to market themselves and their agents accordingly.

With the creation of Online Agent and Online Manager internal designations, John L. Scott has provided its agents with the means of marketing themselves as technologically proficient agents, capable of serving the client through:

- The Internet
- Email
- Agent Homepage
- Digital Photography
- Real Time Marketing

Upon certification, Online Agents and Online Managers earn a certificate of completion which entitles them to use the Online Agent/Manager logo on their business cards and home page.

Most agents are eager to learn about the various technological tools that they can use to enhance their client's real estate experience. The Online Agent and Online Manager designations tap into this excitement and enable agents to market themselves as well-trained professionals in the areas of technology and the Internet. In essence, they become *real time real estate agents.*

'"Anywhere" Infrastructure

Real estate companies need to adapt technology to their agents' work environment. Agents simply do not spend very much time in the office; therefore it's important to have a system in place that allows them to make full use of the company's innovative tools, regardless of where they are working from—office, home, or field. Furthermore, agents must be able to input listing information from locations other than the branch office. Because of this and the importance of *one minute marketing,* real estate companies must develop an infrastructure that enables agents to instantly input listing information from anywhere they have Internet access. In doing so, many agents will express an interest in learning more about innovative applications that they can use with this remote web-based access system—another reason for companies to develop internal designation programs like Online Agent/ Online Manager.

Internet Listing Demo

With the right infrastructure in place, next generation real estate agents have the ability to do much more than just input listings with their remote access capabilities. The tech-savvy agent does real time online demonstrations for potential sellers to illustrate the power of the Internet and real time marketing. For example, agents who have laptop computers with Internet access can perform live Internet listing demos, with virtual tours, audio descriptions and multiple photos. It's really quite simple, but the key is that real estate companies need to develop the necessary infrastructure and training so agents have this opportunity. With a digital camera and laptop computer, an agent can go to a potential listing, take multiple photos of the home, download those photos onto a computer, assign a home web address, create a virtual home tour, write a custom script for the audio description, send it to the voicer, input all of the necessary details, and have the final product in less than one hour. Agents can also utilize the services of a marketing coordinator to organize all of the details from the office and then email the finished package back to the agent. This process also takes under an hour.

The agent can then use the seller's computer or a laptop computer at the listing presentation, in order to do a live demonstration. This type of presentation shows sellers the type of marketing their home will receive. If the seller decides to list with the company, that demo can be immediately turned into a live listing with the simple click of a button. This is truly real-time marketing, and it has an impressive impact on clients during a listing presentation. Agents will win more listings, meet more buyers, and increase their business exponentially if they have access to the tools for this type of presentation. Agents must also be properly trained to provide live Internet demos because to be successful in next generation real estate it is essential to provide day-one marketing.

In next generation real estate, agents will actually be able to provide this type of service to clients without ever stepping foot inside an office. As wireless technology becomes more readily available, agents will have the ability to do everything that was just explained, but from their wireless laptops. The agent will activate this entire process from almost anywhere, including the seller's home, without having to connect to their phone line. Digital cameras with virtual tour capabilities, enable agents to provide real-time virtual tours and eliminate the five-day delay that it currently takes to add a property to an online listing. New cameras with built-in modems will enable agents to immediately upload photos and produce live Internet listing demonstrations in an instant.

Evernet—Always Wired, Always Available

The term *evernet* simply means always being connected to technology and real time information—regardless of a person's whereabouts. Next generation real estate is quickly heading toward the concept of evernet which is evident through incredible technological advances, including enhanced versions of wireless email. For example, in the future, agents will have the option to wear an ear piece that provides voice notification every time a new listing that fits a client's search parameters comes onto the market. The agent will then put on a pair of glasses fitted with small video screens on which photos of the home are projected. If the agent determines it's something that would interest a client, the agent simply states "please send to buyer," and an email is automatically generated and delivered to the buyer. If the buyers approve of the home, they can send a response immediately telling the agent to arrange for a showing—or a purchase and sale agreement. How's that for technology? This might sound extremely high-tech, and it is, but this type of technology is not very far away. This is simply a glimpse into next generation real estate.

BROKER RECIPROCITY
(Internet Data Exchange)

The History of Broker Reciprocity

Broker Reciprocity which is now commonly referred to by the National Association of Realtors as Internet Data Exchange (IDX), is the process of sharing listing information from competing brokers so that companies can display their competitor's inventories on their own web sites. This movement began in 1996 in the Pacific Northwest where John L. Scott Real Estate and other real estate brokerages throughout Washington State partnered to display the entire Northwest Multiple Listing Service inventory on all of their web sites. This process enabled and empowered brokers to be the local portal for real estate information. As a result of Broker Reciprocity, consumers have a local resource from which they can gain comprehensive information about the housing market in their area, regardless of which company's web site they visit. From an industry standpoint, Broker Reciprocity has created an environment of cooperation, rather than competition—or a hybrid of the two that might be called *coopetition*. The actions taken by Pacific Northwest brokerages have set a successful example for the rest of the industry, an example that many across the nation are now following.

Broker Reciprocity has empowered brokers to be the local real estate portal, enhancing the business and service provided to customers. It took a two-minute conversation for the brokers in the Pacific Northwest to decide to implement Broker Reciprocity. They immediately identified the benefits of this program and those anticipated benefits have since surpassed all expectations. The proof is in the numbers: in the Pacific Northwest only 12 percent of homebuyers who use the Internet during their search process go to national real estate web sites— only 12 percent! To further demonstrate this point, it is worth noting that 57 percent of all Internet homebuyers visit John L. Scott Real Estate's web site to gather information during their home search (Hebert Research, 2000). These numbers would not be possible with out Broker Reciprocity.

What it comes down to is that buyers prefer to go to local real estate sites rather than to national portals. Buying and/or selling a home is an extremely personal experience and most home owners want to deal with their local business relationships, not some unknown national web site. The Internet success achieved in the Pacific Northwest would not be possible if not for Broker Reciprocity because buyers would be forced to go to national sites to gather complete information about their local real estate market. This process alone would threaten local relationships and take away much of the local brokers' power. Broker Reciprocity enables brokerages to increase their exposure, not just in their local areas, but nationally, as well. Broker Reciprocity has increased real estate activity exponentially and has allowed companies to provide an enhanced level of customer service that would never be possible without it.

Some companies are skeptical of Broker Reciprocity because they think that by posting their competitors' listings on their web site, they'll lose potential clients. It is time to rethink that idea. The Internet, as explained in chapter 2, is a relationship-based tool. And one of the reasons the Internet is used in real estate is to enhance existing relationships with clients. Real estate companies should not be afraid of losing clients who sees another company's listing on its web site. Those clients are probably there in the first place because they already have some level of a relationship with that particular company. Companies that practice Broker Reciprocity are being of service to their clients by enabling them to visit one place to see photos of every home for sale in the service area. There is substantial value in this because clients are not being forced to go to a competitor's web site to see other listings, nor are they being driven to national web sites. The purpose is to offer everything for them in one centralized online location, so they stay under your company's influence. The same can be said for all brokers who practice Broker Reciprocity.

Broker Reciprocity also enhances marketing abilities because the company can advertise that it has photos of every home for sale on its web site. Yes, the competitors in the area can do this, too, but ultimately it comes down to the investment a company makes in its relationships. Clients will go to the web site of whichever company has been successful in establishing a relationship with them.

Broker Reciprocity provides the opportunity to offer enhanced real time marketing utilizing email notification programs that email clients when any new listing that fits their search parameters comes onto the market, even if it's listed with a competitor. Without this level of service, the individual company is extremely limited and the real estate industry is ultimately weakened. Let's face it, the goal is to find the client's dream home, and that home could be listed with any real estate company, even a competitor's. Broker Reciprocity provides a comprehensive resource from which everyone can access the same information. Buyers with access to this level of information have a better experience, making the overall process more rewarding for all involved.

Ultimately, every buyer should be going through a local broker's web site. The client relationships are with the local broker, so why give away those relationships to a national portal with advertisers who would like to capture the local customers? Brokers have too much invested in their agents, office infrastructure, and technology to have their businesses go through a national site. A company will never again see the client who goes to a national portal. What company wants to pay to send its clients to a national site so they can be redirected to competitors, or back to the company, for a referral fee. It is better to invest in bringing those clients directly to the local broker—no third party involved. This is primarily why the brokers in the Pacific Northwest decided to develop Broker Reciprocity.

Broker Reciprocity is now operating nationwide. Many regions are coming together to offer this same type of service and the results are just as successful as they have been in the Pacific Northwest. However, in some areas, the Multiple Listing Service (MLS) is operating as the local portal for real estate information because the MLS moved more quickly than the broker. This was typically the result of a lack of funds, or lack of understanding about technology, on the part of the broker. But now there are no excuses. Those brokers who are allowing the MLS to be the local portal for real estate information need to develop their own Broker Reciprocity system. While the MLS played an important role, brokers now need to empower themselves to take back their local relationships. It's their brand; they should protect it.

There is so much value in developing Broker Reciprocity. It allows the company to be the local real estate portal for the clients. It increases company web traffic, and it enhances brand identity. Those who do not practice Broker Reciprocity receive one-tenth the web traffic of those who do use it. John L. Scott's web site currently receives over forty-five million hits, including 425,000 unique visitors a month (January, 2002). John L. Scott's traffic ranks as high as some of the national real estate web sites—this most certainly would not be the case without Broker Reciprocity.

What it comes down to is this: the local broker needs to out-dot-com the dot-coms. They must take control of their relationships and their business—not give them away to national real estate portals that end up managing them for a fee. Broker reciprocity empowers real estate companies to out-dot the national real estate dot-coms because they have the local relationships. And no matter how much money they spend, the dot-coms can't come near those relationships.

Some brokers worry about the expense involved in developing Broker Reciprocity. This is a valid concern, but one that's easily put to rest. Nowadays, there are vendors who will implement Broker Reciprocity at a relatively low cost. At John L. Scott, the infrastructure was more costly because several extra components and features were added. These additions are not essential in order to have basic Broker Reciprocity. It's simply up to the brokers and their priorities.

Local brokers will always have an advantage over the national real estate dot-coms because they already have the local relationships and the much-coveted trust factor. The dot-coms are forced to start from square one by establishing relationships, something they weren't counting on when the whole dot-com boom started. Now the brokers are standing tall because they held their ground while the national real estate dot-com companies said they would fail. By combining resources, enhancing relationships, and applying technology, the local brokers will continue to succeed.

National Broker Reciprocity

With Broker Reciprocity well in place on the local level, brokers are now working towards the development of a national Broker Reciprocity system. National Broker Reciprocity would operate from a similar premise, allowing brokers around the country to display links to each other's web sites. National Broker Reciprocity enables the local broker's relationships to have access to information on homes for sale throughout the United States. This is referred to as an industry portal because it is controlled by the local broker, not Wall Street. With national Broker Reciprocity on the verge of becoming a reality, exciting opportunities lie ahead for brokers.

Currently, national real estate portals, such as Realtor.com and HomeAdvisor.com, are the main sites that are able to post national listing inventories. Therefore, if customers in Washington State want to view homes for sale in Vermont, they must go through sites, such as Realtor.com and HomeAdvisor.com to find the local broker's listings. Realtor.com has been a tremendous asset to many brokers, however, now the time has come to thank them for their service and to develop an independent system that allows the local broker to operate as the industry portal. As discussed earlier, the local broker has the local relationships, not the national web sites. Because of this, clients who are in search of a home want to work through their local brokerage, not a national site. This is evident through the statistics quoted earlier that stated only 12 percent of homebuyers in the Pacific Northwest go to national real estate web sites to do a home search. And with national Broker Reciprocity in place, local agencies will absorb most of those remaining buyers who are currently using national portals to search for a home.

With national Broker Reciprocity in place, companies can act as that local portal of information, even if buyers are looking for a home outside of their local geographic region. In essence, the local company introduces buyers to the local brokers in the area to which they are moving. There is intrinsic value in this process because the clients are able to establish new relationships through the broker with whom they already have a trusted relationship. With this system, there is no need for the third party relationship involving a national site.

The RELO® network recently launched a program that enables brokers to offer national search functionality on their company web sites. This program is the first step towards implementing national Broker Reciprocity. Unlike national real estate portals, the RELO® program offers property inventory which is updated daily and is housed on the local broker's web site.

Another benefit of the RELO® program is the enhanced referral system that results from having relationships with participating brokers across the United States. Too often, consumers moving to another area select a real estate professional arbitrarily, rather than obtaining a reliable recommendation. By helping clients begin their search locally, brokers not only can provide valuable early information, but they can also make an introduction to a qualified real estate professional at the destination. This type of service makes a significant difference in the entire relocation experience.

In January, 2002 John L. Scott became the first broker in the Pacific Northwest to join the RELO® program and implement national search capabilities on the company web site. Now the John L. Scott site features hundreds of thousands of homes from across the country, with additional properties being added on an ongoing basis. This is in addition to the entire Northwest Multiple Listing Service, which is already accessible on John L. Scott's web site.

To access the national search function on a participating broker's web site, visitors select "National Search" on the broker's home page. The visitor is then able to select the appropriate destination area and price range. From here they have immediate access to comprehensive property information for that area. For additional details, they can request assistance from the broker's customer service department. Applying the same services available to corporate transferees, the broker will refer the customer to a pre-screened real estate professional in the new area and will monitor the service delivery process to ensure that the customer's needs are met.

Ultimately the local broker should be the one establishing and maintaining relationships with consumers in their local markets. Companies need to support efforts to keep those relationships local instead of sending them out into the national dot-com abyss. Doing so will bulletproof the agent's relationships, improve business and enhance the customer's entire real estate experience.

4

TRANSACTION MANAGEMENT

Next generation real estate is all about taking traditional real estate processes and bringing them into the age of technology. The purpose for doing this is to enhance the level of customer service for clients and to make the overall real estate process more efficient for all involved. An area of real estate that is quickly evolving because of technology is transaction management. The next generation real estate company uses online transaction management software—an online software system that streamlines the entire transaction process.

Real estate agents have three primary functions: customer relationship management, business development, and real estate transactions. Unfortunately the transaction process demands an enormous amount of an agent's time and attention, forcing the agent to focus less on other primary functions. This demand often upsets an agent's balance of life. Traditionally, real estate agents have managed the various stages of the transaction themselves, and for many, this is the least appealing part about being an agent because it's extremely time consuming. As a result, many top producing agents hire personal assistants to handle transaction management for them. This leaves the agents free to focus on what they're best at—representing clients. The use of transaction coordinators is a serious paradigm shift in the traditional structure of real estate and it may even be a difficult adjustment for some agents. However, the implementation of online transaction management is one of the greatest breakthroughs in agent productivity in the history of real estate. This is why.

Online transaction management provides one centralized online location for every aspect of the transaction, from the purchase and sale agreement to the property inspection, appraisal, lender approval, and title and escrow work. The various steps involved in the transaction process are managed by transaction coordinators, hired professionals who charge on a per transaction basis. It's similar in concept to having a personal assistant, but without the full-time expense. Additionally, the cost of hiring a transaction coordinator is minimal compared to the overall commission that an agent receives. For example, in many cases, agents only pay $150 per transaction for transaction coordinator services. Agents still act as their client's advocates, but by using a transaction coordinator, they no longer have to manage the intricate day-to-day details of the transaction. It frees them of one of the most time-consuming aspects of the entire real estate process and allows them to apply that time toward other areas of their business.

Transaction services are affordable. *All* agents can use them because the cost is figured on a per-transaction fee, compared to the expense of a full-time assistant. For agents who already have assistants, using a transaction coordinator allows those assistants to increase their focus on other revenue-producing priorities, such as business development and customer relationship management. Transaction services are one of the greatest additions to real estate because they enable agents to have it all: more transactions, more personal time and more balance of life.

Online transaction management software also enhances the customer experience because clients have constant access to updates on their transactions. Studies show that buyers and sellers want this level of communication during their real estate transaction. In fact, after the purchase and sale agreement is signed most have indicated that they want daily communication. It contributes to their excitement level and appeases any fears they might have. Buying or selling a home is a major financial commitment, and clients want to know about the status of their transaction every step of the way. This can be very demanding of agents who are working in the field, tending to other clients. Online transactions empower both the agents and clients.

Online transaction software links every aspect of the transaction to one centralized, online location, allowing all parties involved to view information on an as-needed basis. (The information is password protected.) Agents are always their client's primary information source, but they can also choose to have their clients receive email notification or phone calls from the transaction coordinator whenever significant events are updated on their transaction. Clients have reported that the lack of communication during the transaction process is one of their largest dissatisfactions, so the enhanced communication aspect is a great benefit. Online transaction software also eliminates much of the duplication that takes place between the mortgage, title, and escrow processes, reducing the overall transaction process time significantly. Furthermore, the transaction is managed by a professional who is trained specifically in transaction management, reducing the margin for error and providing reassurance for all involved.

As mentioned earlier, there are agents who will be resistant to the use of transaction coordinators because they believe they are already successfully managing everything themselves, including the transaction process. While those feelings are understandable, agents need to learn the importance of remaining focused on their primary responsibilities.

The following story illustrates this point.

When I was seventeen years old, my father taught me a very important lesson about trying to take on too many responsibilities. It happened when I was an Eagle Scout attending an International Boy Scout Jamboree in Japan. I was a patrol leader, responsible for coordinating tasks and chores of my eight-member patrol. One morning I woke early and decided to build the fire for breakfast. My father was an adult Scout leader for our troop at the Jamboree. Upon seeing me building the fire, my father asked me what I was doing. He followed this by asking me what my job as a patrol leader was. I responded by telling him that my job was to coordinate the patrol. He then asked whose job it was to build the fire. I told him whose responsibility it was and that since I was up early and the Scout responsible for building the fire was just waking up, I decided to lend a hand. At that point, my dad laid it on the line for me, he asked, "Do you want to be the patrol leader or do you want to be the person who builds fires?" At that moment it became very clear to me what he was saying. Dad was teaching me that being the leader of the group does not mean you do all the tasks yourself, but rather you delegate them to others so that together you can function as a team. My responsibility as patrol leader was to coordinate the activities and I could not do this effectively if I was taking on other Scout's jobs.

Every real estate agent is faced with the same type of decision: Is the agent going to be a real estate consultant or a transaction coordinator? The answer should be easy.

Those agents who feel they can do it all need to realize that using a transaction coordinator can free up over 30 percent of their time. This valuable time can be applied toward business development, customer relationship management or more personal time away from work.

Agents who hire transaction coordinators are able to double their productivity and have more balanced lives. Furthermore, by delegating the responsibilities of the transaction to a coordinator, agents are elevated to consultant status and are able to manage their business more efficiently.

Transaction coordinators provide a service that enhances the customer's experience as well. The transaction process itself takes less time to complete and customers are kept in constant communication regarding the status of their transaction. The use of transaction coordinators and online transaction management software will result in more satisfied customers and repeat referral business—the greatest compliment to any real estate professional.

Transaction Service Center
Building A New Stadium

The real estate industry would do well to follow the lead of many major league baseball teams that are building new ballparks to increase revenue for purposes of reinvestment in their future. The new facility enables them to compete at the highest level and puts them in a better position to win championships.

Real estate companies, just like ball teams, need economic revenue to be successful. They cannot rely on the small margin they receive from agent commissions, and must find alternative methods to gain the funding they need to implement next generation real estate.

The future success of the real estate industry relies on economic development. Customers and agents want powerful companies, tools, and services, but these things cannot be obtained without adequate revenue and profits. Transaction service centers will provide the opportunity for additional real estate revenue, enabling companies to invest and reinvest in future success.

Client Transaction Services

Real estate companies are realizing that customers want *one stop shopping* when it comes to their real estate needs. Because of this, next generation real estate companies must provide and coordinate all services from one location. Clients look to their agents for recommended service providers—something that can easily be made available when the services are all housed in one location. Because buying or selling a home is one of the biggest financial transactions of a person's life, many clients want all aspects of their transaction handled together by one trusted company. This is why it will be essential for real estate companies to develop transaction service centers.

A transaction service center houses offices for all facets of real estate transaction services, including transaction coordinators and escrow, title, and mortgage representatives. It incorporates all the individual services that make up a real estate transaction. This type of service center allows companies to focus on what they are good at—selling real estate—while hiring experts to fulfill the other operations (mortgage, title, escrow). It's really just a reshuffling of the deck. These various professionals currently exist at other companies. So, next generation real estate companies merely need to bring them together and centralize their operations in one location to make it easier for agents and clients. Agents are already consulting their clients about all aspects of home ownership so it seems appropriate for real estate companies to expand their offerings to include these client transaction services.

John L. Scott Real Estate strongly believes that transaction management is the answer to higher productivity. Because of this, the company recently opened its own transaction service center called

TranServ. TranServ relocated transaction coordinators from various John L. Scott offices so that they could operate in one centralized location, providing all-agent access to these services. There are a few exceptions in which John L. Scott chose to leave coordinators in the company's larger metro-area offices because they have the volume to support in-house transaction coordination.

TranServ also houses the John L. Scott title and escrow operations, further streamlining the transaction process because the coordinators can literally walk across the hall to communicate with one another and facilitate paperwork. This enables them to manage the transactions more efficiently, which helps lower the cost of the transaction fee charged to the agents, and makes the services accessible to everyone. It is also a benefit to those offices that are not large enough to support in-house transaction coordinators because they now have access to these services, too.

Those companies that do not take the progressive step toward implementing transaction services ultimately will not be able to compete with companies that do. The harsh reality is that the real estate industry does not make a fair return to the brokers. These days agents keep as much as 75 to 85 percent or more of the commission revenue they bring into the company, leaving little income for brokerages to invest in their future. Far too many brokers and agents suffer because the broker cannot afford to keep up with the costs associated with providing the ultimate level of customer service. By creating opportunities for revenue sources, the local broker will be able to compete and succeed. Client transaction services can provide these revenues, bringing value to the broker and the agent. Companies are in partnership with their agents and the development of client transaction services enhances both groups' ability to be successful. Ultimately, the result is a win for the agent, a win for the company, and most importantly, a win for the customer.

5

ENHANCING THE HOME OWNERSHIP EXPERIENCE^{sm}

The real estate industry is an exciting place to be right now. Modern technology is rapidly changing real estate marketing, communication and transaction processes, yet the fundamental principles continue to drive the business and create opportunities. To achieve optimal success in real estate, agents need to utilize these technological advances without losing sight of what's most important—trusted client relationships.

Success in next generation real estate revolves around a philosophy I call *enhancing the home ownership experience*, which enhances the agent-client relationship throughout the client's *entire* home ownership experience.

Home ownership is a cycle that continues throughout a client's life, and includes buying, selling, and living in the home. Real estate companies should prepare their agents to provide services to their clients through all stages of this home ownership experience. This enables agents to remain in contact with their clients, enhancing the client's home ownership experience, and leading to repeat business and referrals for the agents.

Providing these enhanced services should not be limited to current home owners. Agents should establish relationships with future home owners as well. This can be done by communicating about what's involved in being a first time home buyer, by helping them evaluate their financial position, and by advising them on the best time to begin looking. By establishing this relationship and providing them with quality service *before* they are home owners, the agent creates a long-term client relationship and subsequent referrals.

Home Services

The home ownership enhancement philosophy is based on the premise that everything in the business is driven by the goal of customer enhancement. Home buyers, sellers, and owners have different needs because they are in different stages of the home ownership cycle. Therefore, companies need to offer services that address all these experiences. The idea is to treat each client as a valued individual and to meet individual client needs accordingly. A program that John L. Scott Real Estate recently introduced, called John L. Scott Home Services, equips agents with the information and tools they need to assist their current and existing clients with these enhanced home services.

There are currently several examples of home services type programs in place across the United States, but many real estate companies still do not offer this level of customer service. This service will be vital to success in next generation real estate, because the clients will come to expect it.

Most home services programs include both property transfer services and home ownership services.

Property transfer services involve utility connections, address change notification, mail forwarding, moving company contacts, voter registration, drivers license changes, and storage facility arrangements.

Because the utility transfer and hookup process can be very time consuming and stressful, one of the most valuable aspects of the home services program is the utility connection service, which helps clients change or establish utility services in the new home.

Home ownership services address the needs of home owners while they are living in their home. These services include yard maintenance, cleaning services, and home improvement contractor connections. By establishing professional relationships with preferred service providers, agents can provide clients with valuable discounts that will save them time and money. In this way, the agent will become the clients' single point of contact for all home ownership needs—ultimately enhancing the agent-client relationship.

To facilitate a successful home services program, real estate companies must develop business relationships with vendors, including moving companies, home maintenance contractors and storage facility companies. In most cases, the vendors pay to market themselves to the clients because it provides an enormous return benefit for them. In essence, the broker is the distribution channel through which vendors can market themselves to certain home ownership groups, resulting in increased business for them and enhanced service for the customers.

By offering a home services program, agents are able to provide their clients with a more complete overall service package that assists them with every stage of home ownership. Studies show that real estate clients use their agent's service recommendations 80 to 90 percent of the time, clearly demonstrating that they want agents to provide them with this type of service. Forty-two percent of home owners surveyed said that they want a resource for home improvement specialists. Simply put, clients don't want to deal with locating vendors, and often refer to their agents for recommendations. They look to their agents as experts on all things related to home ownership. Despite these figures, only 24 percent of real estate agents nation-wide are currently providing their clients with this type of information (National Association of Realtors, 2001).

Every agent has been in a position of having no referral available for a client who needed one. With a home services program in place, agents and their clients have direct access to service providers in many areas of home ownership. This removes the pressure from the agent and results in a high level of client satisfaction.

With a home services program in place, the services are conveniently facilitated and managed for the agent. Some agents have existing relationships with service providers and will choose to continue to use them. However, many agents have not established such relationships. This type of program provides a centralized resource for agents to access so that they may provide their clients with valuable contacts and information.

There are different approaches to managing the client contact through a home services type program. Some are managed through individual offices, and others operate primarily online or through a third party. John L. Scott wanted to manage its own system so a web site was created that is an extension of the company's primary web site (www.homeservices.johnlscott.com). This web site enables John L. Scott agents and clients to have direct access to home ownership services. Everything is arranged by zip code so agents and clients can easily find the services and providers available in their areas, and the clients are contacted directly by those vendors. The vendors are subjected to an extremely thorough screening process to ensure that clients receive the highest quality service.

Home Warranties

Another service that is very valuable to home buyers and sellers is home warranty coverage. In 2000, about 20 percent of the homes purchased nationwide were covered by a home warranty. The average number of claims per warranty was about one-and-a-half. The number of home warranties is increasing every year because home owners are becoming more informed about the benefits. A survey in the Pacific Northwest indicated that 59.4 percent of recent home buyers would have liked to have been offered the option of a home warranty (Hebert Research, 2000). Because of this, it is extremely wise for real estate companies to develop relationships with home warranty companies so that agents may offer their clients the benefit of a home warranty. There are different levels of service that home warranty companies offer, but in some instances this type of relationship results in the exclusive ability to provide home sellers with free home warranty coverage during the term of their listing. This valuable service provides insurance in the event of unforeseen home repairs on selected home appliances, enhancing the real estate experience enormously.

Beyond the free listing coverage, home sellers are typically given the opportunity to purchase a one year policy for the buyer of their home. The cost of the policy is paid at closing. Again, in most cases, if the clients choose not to purchase this extended policy, they sign a waiver form stating so. The purpose of this is to reduce the liability for the agent if something should go wrong with the home, post sale. Most importantly, the perception of liability is lessened. For example, if something goes wrong that would have been insured by a home warranty and the client has signed a waiver declining coverage, the weight of responsibility is seemingly removed from the agent. The client made a conscious choice not to purchase a home warranty. Therefore, in most cases, the agent will not be held liable.

Often when a situation arises, it is the result of an inspection oversight, but in many instances the perception by the client is that it's the agent's fault. Imagine after spending several months working through a successful transaction with the client to have a perfectly pleasant relationship ruined by a broken-down dishwasher. With a home warranty in place, the agent avoids a potential conflict with the client, and the client is elated to only be paying a service fee for a brand new dishwasher. The agent-client relationship has been protected, and chances are the satisfied client will refer the agent to others.

A home warranty offers many advantages to the home seller and buyer, the least of which is piece of mind knowing that major home appliances are covered in the event of a breakdown.

Most home warranties cover both parts and labor of a home's most vital systems and major appliances. This protects the home seller from unexpected repair bills and also allows the buyer to purchase the home with more confidence. Additionally, a home warranty is usually for the term of at least one year, so any unforeseen repairs or replacements are also covered well after the home has been sold. As mentioned, this is a relief for agents because they are no longer the point of contact for dissatisfied clients who have unexpected home repairs. With a home warranty in place, that responsibility is diverted to the home warranty company. A home warranty also provides a competitive edge over those listings without warranties because it communicates confidence to buyers. There is no question that sellers get their money's worth, and the fee is part of the closing costs, so it's very manageable. This can add up to a faster selling period, resulting in a more pleasing, convenient process for all involved.

6

CUSTOMER RELATIONSHIP MANAGEMENT

To be successful in real estate, it's extremely important to establish a long-term relationship with clients throughout the home ownership experience. This can be done successfully by practicing Customer Relationship Management (CRM). CRM is the perpetuation and ongoing communication between agent and client that works to deepen and maintain customer loyalty. It involves the contact agents have with their sphere of influence, which includes past, current, and potentially-future clients. Chapter five described the need for real estate companies to develop home services programs to provide customers with enhanced services, such as property transfer and home improvement. CRM takes this approach even further by using content-rich, client-specific, information to facilitate ongoing dialogue between agents and their clients. History has proven that highly satisfied clients will typically communicate their experience to others—potentially resulting in increased referral business and a major productivity boost for agents. All of this clearly illustrates the importance of practicing CRM.

Research has shown that homeowners want continued communication with their agents after the transaction is complete and they are living in their home. More specifically, they have indicated that they want their agents to provide them with information relevant to their personal home ownership experience. In a recent survey of new homeowners in the Pacific Northwest, 73 percent stated that they wanted their agents to provide them with an annual updated value of their homes. Sixty- eight percent indicated they would like their agents to keep in touch with them about refinancing, and 42 percent said they would like to receive home equity information. In addition to this, 54 percent of home owners said they wanted to receive some form of neighborhood news, and 60 percent indicated that they would appreciate receiving seasonal home maintenance information. (Hebert Research, 2000.)

Through CRM, agents can provide services and information, such as these, enhancing the client's individual home ownership experience. For example, some agents provide annual home value updates so their clients have the most current information for taxes, insurance and financial investments. Additionally, they can provide current interest rates and mortgage information to determine if refinancing is a viable option. Clients have also indicated that they appreciate receiving information about new listings on homes in their neighborhoods. This helps to keep the homeowners aware of the state of the current housing market in their areas.

An agent that practices CRM might also send clients reminders of seasonal home maintenance suggestions, such as when it is the best time to have gutters cleaned or the deck stained. Another useful service is to send clients a calendar of community events.

CRM allows agents to send very targeted information to niches within their client base. It can even get specific to the person's individual lifestyle, for example, clients who enjoy gardening could receive information about seasonal rose care or notification that the home and garden show is coming to town. This is all information that customers have indicated they want to receive from their agents. In essence, they have given agents permission to provide them with this type of information; in some cases, they've outright asked for it. By providing this level of service, agents enhance and deepen the relationship with their clients.

CRM is an essential investment because it will lead to a giant productivity boost for agents. CRM has proven to generate repeat and referral business; it's simply in people's nature to tell others in their own sphere of influence when they are happy with the service they're receiving. A person's sphere of influence can include an array of people from business associates to family members, friends, clients—anyone with whom they might have contact. The point is that all satisfied clients have the potential to convey their experiences to those with whom they come into contact. CRM significantly increases an agent's ability to enhance the client's experience and receive increased business because of it.

It is important to note that CRM is not designed to be obtrusive or to spam clients with information. Rather, it's about having permission from the clients to provide them with enhanced service. Twenty-three percent of homeowners surveyed in the Pacific Northwest said that they want annual contact from their agents, 20 percent every six months, and 21 percent indicated they would like to hear from their agents quarterly. Nine percent said they'd like contact from their agents once a month; 8 percent said they wanted to be contacted only as new, valuable information came about and 8 percent didn't have an answer. Only 11 percent said they didn't want any contact with their agent at all (Hebert Research, 2000).

This ongoing contact is supported by the one-on-one relationship that agents have with their clients and the trust that those clients place in their agents. As a part of this program, it's important to have a privacy policy that assures agents and clients that a client's information will not be shared with anyone, and will only be used for the purpose of CRM.

Two important books about customer relationship management are *Permission Marketing*, by Seth Godin (Seth Godin, Adapted by Don Peppers/Simon & Schuster Trade/April 1999), and *Swim with the Sharks Without Being Eaten Alive*, by Harvey MacKay (Harvey MacKay, Foreword by Kenneth Blanchard/Random House, Incorporated /February 1989).

Next Generation Contact Management Software

Technology has increased communication and customer service capabilities immensely. Because of these advancements in technology real estate companies can use contact management software specifically for CRM. Contact management software provides client information that goes far beyond names and addresses. Through this software, agents have access to information such as the type of home in which an individual lives and the features of that home (such as wood floors, carpet and types of appliances). Agents can also track whether or not the clients have a garden and if so, if gardening is their hobby. The software can provide access to construction details, such as the type of siding or kind of roof. Basically any details that are specific to that particular home and its owners is information that is available through contact management software.

Contact management software also enables agents to communicate with individuals about relevant, important events that are taking place in their area. For example, the West Coast power crisis in 2001, offered the perfect opportunity for agents to practice CRM by providing clients with information about energy conservation in the home. John L. Scott Real Estate did just that by creating an energy efficiency flyer for agents to distribute to clients. They also added an "Energy Tips" page to their web site and partnered with local utility companies to distribute coupons for Energy Star appliances and free CFL light bulbs. Many home owners already look to their real estate agents as the authority on home ownership, but CRM services such as these made available through contact management software, provide additional credibility, and contribute to enhancement of the clients' home ownership experience.

You may be wondering how and what type of information is gathered. In order to facilitate successful CRM, companies need to partner with their agents and create effective ways that agents can attain this information. CRM is only as good as the client-specific data that is gathered. The primary way to facilitate this is to have agents simply ask their clients basic questions. Following is a comprehensive list of the type of information an agent could potentially gather from their clients:

A. House Information:
    a. Home anniversary
    b. MLS listing information
    c. Type of house
    d. Style of house
    e. Special niche (such as a waterfront; or acreage location)
    f. Siding (type; percentage of house covered; trim)
    g. Flooring materials
    h. Appliances
    i. Years remaining on roof
    j. Yard (size; type)
    k. Hot tub, rose garden, lawn, fountain
    l. Home equity line
    m. Mortgage, refinancing
    n. Home owner warranty
    o. Home owner insurance

    p. Emergency contacts
    q. Drainage, structure, utilities
    r. Value of property
    s. Neighborhood information (schools, churches, emergency services, crime rate)

B. Personal Information:
    a. Areas of interest
    b. Hobbies
    c. Birthdays
    d. Anniversaries
    e. Miscellaneous information

Simply knowing that the client enjoys gardening opens a host of communication topics, such as seasonal garden care, gardening events, and garden care companies in the area. Any aspect of a person's home ownership has the potential for this type of follow up. The agent just needs to get to know their clients' preferences and needs. The key is to have one-on-one communication with each client, based on the information that is relevant to each client's lifestyle. As far as distribution of information is concerned, one study indicated the following for preferred methods of delivery:

Email	35%
Letter	26.5%
Newsletter	25%
Postcard	16.5%

Mass mailings simply won't cut it. In the future, contacts will need to be tailored to the individuals through their preferred channels of distribution.

Many agents feel they simply do not have the time to facilitate CRM practices. Some have even purchased contact management software, but never found the time to use it. This is a common complaint and as a result, CRM often takes a back seat to other perceived priorities such as transaction management and marketing. This reinforces the importance of a partnership between real estate companies and their agents. In the past, it was up to agents to manage their own CRM, however next generation real estate is about companies empowering their agents to succeed by supporting their CRM efforts. In order to do this, companies need to take on the administrative side and facilitate CRM by managing the agent's client profiles. The relationship remains between the agents and their clients and no contact is ever made with clients unless the agent approves.

There are several phases to establishing and managing CRM. One is to create a client database using information gathered by the agents. In phase two these clients are divided into different groups based on home style, location, zip code, etc. Once the client base has been categorized, the company can begin facilitating communication by sending agents useful information that they can pass along to their sphere of influence. The agents are always the point of contact for their clients. The company acts as a support system by managing the client/agent CRM database and emailing agents information they can use to maintain relationships with their customers. This frees agents of the time-consuming process of managing their clients' individual profiles and provides them with detailed information and marketing materials that they can use to facilitate regular contact with clients.

National real estate speaker Brian Buffini travels the country talking about the advantages and success in practicing CRM. His highly successful approach to CRM has been well received and greatly praised by real estate professionals across the nation. Brian advises agents to break their clients into four distinct groups. Group A includes those who will employ you if they have a need for real estate services and who also have the personality type to refer you to others. Group B includes those who will use your real estate services if they have a need. Group C consists of potential clients who can be matured into groups A or B. Group D includes those with whom the agent chooses not to work. They are dealt with professionally, then deleted from the client base.

Groups A and B are the ones from which agents receive the most return, and are therefore worth the most CRM investment. Not to discount group C—this group could be potential group A or group B clients as the agent/client relationship builds.

Here is how CRM software works into this scenario. If prompted, CRM software can inform agents each month about which clients are approaching their annual anniversaries in their homes. The group managing the CRM database emails the agent to let them know their client's anniversary is approaching and that they should consider contacting them to provide the client with a market update on the value of their home. Agents can provide this type of service for any group of clients, but because performing a market update requires a personal visit, many agents reserve this type of service for group A clients.

It is this type of customer service that leads to highly satisfied clients and repeat, referral business.

The entire purpose of CRM is to enable real estate agents to maintain contact within their sphere of influence in order to increase business. Agents are able to build a deeper book of business with complete profiles of their clients, not just a list of names and phone numbers. By practicing CRM, agents are also able to set the stage for continued communication and keeping that very important relationship established with clients.

CRM relies heavily on email and postal mailings. However, relationships fade away without voice-to-voice communication. Without personal visits and voice communication the relationship will inevitably disappear, even with mailings. Studies show that 60 percent of homebuyers forget their agent's name within six months because their agent did not follow through with any type of correspondence. This clearly demonstrates the importance of CRM. Real estate relies entirely on customer relationships, so the function of CRM is *mission critical* to survival and success in this business.

7

LIFE PLAN: THE MOST IMPORTANT CHAPTER

In any profession it's easy for individuals to become so consumed by their careers that perspective is lost, causing life to become unbalanced. Unfortunately this is all too common in the real estate profession and often results in agents becoming burned out. Real estate is a very demanding career that requires considerable time and sustained energy for success. A very important element of that success needs to be proper preparation of a life plan.

To be successful in next generation real estate, it's vitally important for an agent to have a business plan, but even more importantly, the agent needs to develop a life plan. Real estate companies must do their part to support their agents in this process by partnering with them in the development of life plans. In this business it is common to see successful agents who are so wrapped up in their careers that they don't take time to enjoy life. There are also new agents who are so focused on accomplishing their goals that they lose perspective of everything else in their lives. Neither scenario is healthy and both will eventually result in a very nonfulfilling life. Some agents don't give themselves permission to take a day off or a vacation. These same agents often think that this warrants some kind of special acknowledgment, but that is not the case. It simply isn't healthy to operate this way, and managers should work with their agents to help them maintain balance.

A life plan refers to a person's entire life, of which the professional aspect is only one component. Not to be confused with a business plan, a life plan addresses the different elements of an individual's personal life, such as:

- Spiritual Growth
- Personal Growth
- Physical Health
- Personal Relationships
- Parenting
- Powerful Work Experience
- Passion In Life
- Personal Finances
- Philanthropy
- Responsibility To Future Generations
- Community Contributions
- Environmental Protection

What's important to think about when developing a life plan is where the work life should fit in. Work life should be considered the economic engine for a life plan. When work life is fulfilled the individual is able to make money and build personal confidence, which transfers to the other areas of life. It works in the other direction too; as one gains confidence in the other areas of life, the work life will benefit. Because there are so many different aspects to any one person's life, it is important to organize those areas according to priority, so as to have a healthy balance. By doing so, the individual is better able to gain perspective and create an underlying purpose that provides life with an overall direction.

A life plan encourages people to set goals and develop affirmations. It communicates a sense of purpose and fosters positive thoughts and perspectives. The awareness level is enhanced for those who have life plans because they are always working toward something within their plans. People who develop life plans are more organized and able to move toward their goals more quickly. With a life plan in place one can achieve greater things and have more time for a balanced life.

The motivation comes from looking deeply within to the underlying purpose in life, as opposed to looking to outside factors for motivation. When individuals take the time to organize the vital areas of their lives, their focus is clearer and their outlook more positive. People with positive attitudes gravitate toward other people with positive attitudes. Furthermore, it takes less energy to achieve goals and move through life with a positive focus.

So how does this relate to real estate? Having a life plan allows real estate professionals to accomplish more in life, including the work life. It also has the potential to enhance relationships, both personal and professional. Having a life plan creates excitement that is reflected in interactions with

NEXT GENERATION REAL ESTATE

business associates and clients. A life plan ultimately provides the tools to accomplish success in next generation real estate and in all areas of life.

Before developing a successful life plan there are several factors to consider. First and foremost, each person needs to ask, "What would I like to accomplish in life?" Everyone should have some idea of what they want to accomplish in life, whether it's personally, professionally, or both. The answer to this question will provide the direction needed to develop the objectives in a life plan. To do this successfully, it's essential to have an understanding of who one is and to identify the personal requirements for happiness. People who don't have a proper understanding of who they are tend to be unhappy, and they usually have a difficult time determining what they really want from life. In beginning the life plan process, the following questions should be considered:

- What do I want?
- What do I want to see?
- What do I want to be?
- What kind of person do I want to become?
- What is my purpose in life?
- What do I want to have?
- Where do I want to go?
- What would I like to share?
- What is working in my life and what isn't?
- What gets in my way?

Another way to go about this is to develop a *want list*, made up of the eight highest priorities in your life. Making such a list will help uncover the answers to the previous questions.

Life is full of change; therefore a life plan should reflect change. The life plan developed at age twenty-five will probably be different by age forty. The fundamental elements stay the same, but priorities shift depending on which stage in the life cycle has been reached. A life plan is best developed when one is young because it provides strategic planning for the rest of that individual's life.

It's worthwhile to reexamine the life plan every year to keep sight of one's goals. The life plan will evolve a great deal over the years, but it's important to have constant direction and a plan from which to continually work.

Suggested reading for anyone interested in learning more about the benefits of having a life plan is *The On Purpose Person* by Kevin W. McCarthy (Navpress Publishing Group, 1992). This book serves as a great resource for life plan development information. The following is an excerpt from the book:

> Once there was a very successful person. In fact, he was more than successful: his life had meaning and purpose. He knew he was using his time on earth to make a significant difference in other people's lives. He had come to terms with himself, he accepted his strengths as well as his weaknesses. He tried hard to be a better person. He understood, appreciated, and loved many people. People were drawn to him—whether family, friends, business associates, or casual acquaintances.

But it hadn't always been that way. He still carried the memories of those years of frustration when his life had no purpose or foundation. Back then, "living" was just going through the motions, stretched out along a string of days spent reacting to circumstances and people who called the shots for him. He was not in control of his life.

That was many years ago. Things were different now. He had learned a great deal since then. And what he had learned he put into practice—on purpose.

CONCLUDING NOTES FROM THE AUTHOR

My life plan has evolved a great deal over the years, but the underlying principals have primarily remained the same. Personally, my life plan revolves around several key areas, including spiritual growth and personal growth, both of which are greatly influenced by my personal relationships, my love for my family and friends, and keeping healthy. Another very important aspect of my life plan is being successful. Success in my life is defined by how I raise my children, by having the ability to connect with others in a meaningful way, and by being productive in my personal and professional life. It's also very important to me to contribute to my community by teaching future generations, helping those in need, and by doing my part to protect the environment. My favorite word is *possibility* because possibility gives me the freedom to explore and seek out additional information before committing—possibility exists within every aspect of my life plan.

Having a life plan is something I believe so strongly in, that at John L. Scott Real Estate we are offering seminars to our agents to help them develop their life plan plans. Unfortunately, very few of us were taught about life plans in school, so it's important for managers and other real estate leaders to teach agents about their importance. I am in partnership for success with the agents in my company, therefore I make it a priority to provide them with the resources they need to achieve their goals. Developing and sustaining a life plan is a very important element of success and something that all real estate agents and their brokers should aspire to achieve together.

ABOUT THE AUTHOR

J. Lennox Scott is president of John L. Scott Real Estate. Lennox is the third generation to run the family business, which was founded in 1931 by his grandfather, John L. Scott. Upon the passing of his father, W. Lennox Scott, Lennox started in the real estate industry in 1976 at the age of twenty-three and became President in 1980. In 2000, Lennox was recognized by *Realtor® Magazine* as one of the nation's top twenty-five most influential people in real estate. He was also honored in 2001 as one of the top five most admired individuals in real estate in the nation, by *REAL Trends*. Both honors were attributed to Lennox's forward-thinking approach to and use of technology in real estate.

NEXT GENERATION REAL ESTATE

John L. Scott Real Estate has 108 offices with over 2,800 hundred sales associates in the states of Washington, Oregon and Idaho—and a marketing partnership in Maui, Hawaii. In 2000 John L. Scott closed over 41,000 transactions for more than 7.8 billion dollars in volume. *REAL Trends* subsequently ranked John L. Scott Real Estate as the fourth largest regional real estate brand in the United States.

John L. Scott's web site, www.johnlscott.com, is one of the top-rated real estate web sites in the nation and has been a three-time finalist for the Real Estate Connect Internet Innovation Award. John L. Scott's web site has the entire Multiple Listing Inventory in the Northwest and receives over forty-five million hits a month, including 425,000 unique visitors.

Please send:

_____ copies of NEXT GENERATION REAL ESTATE

at $9.95 each   TOTAL   _____

Nebr. residents add 5% sales tax   _____

Shipping/Handling

    $4.50 for first book.

    $.50 for each additional book.   _____

TOTAL ENCLOSED   _____

Name _____

Address _____

City _____ State _____ Zip _____

☐ VISA   ☐ MasterCard   ☐ Discover

Credit card number _____

Expiration date _____

Order by credit card, personal check or money order.

Send to:

Dageforde Publishing, Inc.
128 East 13th Street
Crete, Nebraska 68333

1-800-216-8794
FAX:402-826-4059
ORDER ONLINE AT www.dageforde.com

NOTES